my BIG name

A story about the power of your name

Amonge Sinxoto
Illustrations by **Lebogang Thato Sekwelenkwe**

I am **Isenguye Owakhe Sinxoto**.

This is a story about my **BIG** name, and my first week at **BIG** school.

The night before school starts, I'm so excited I can hardly sleep!

In the morning, I wake up super early. I don't want to be late for my first **BIG** day!

Dad is on hair duty. I want **BIG** Afro puffs.

I have breakfast with my **BIG** family. Mom makes a **BIG** breakfast with waffles, bacon, eggs ...

I arrive at school very early. Mom walks me to my classroom. She gives me a **BIG** kiss and a **BIG** hug, and then she says goodbye.

That's when I notice there are no other children in the classroom ... I was so excited for **BIG** school that I'm the first one here!

My teacher comes over to greet me.
She is so nice. Her name is Teacher Jess.
I tell her my name is **Isenguye**.

She says, "I-seee-gu-umm ... I-sin-goo-ya ...
Wow, this is a really funny name!

I think we'll just call you **Izzy**."

I didn't know I would get a new name
in **BIG** school.

I really like my old name ...

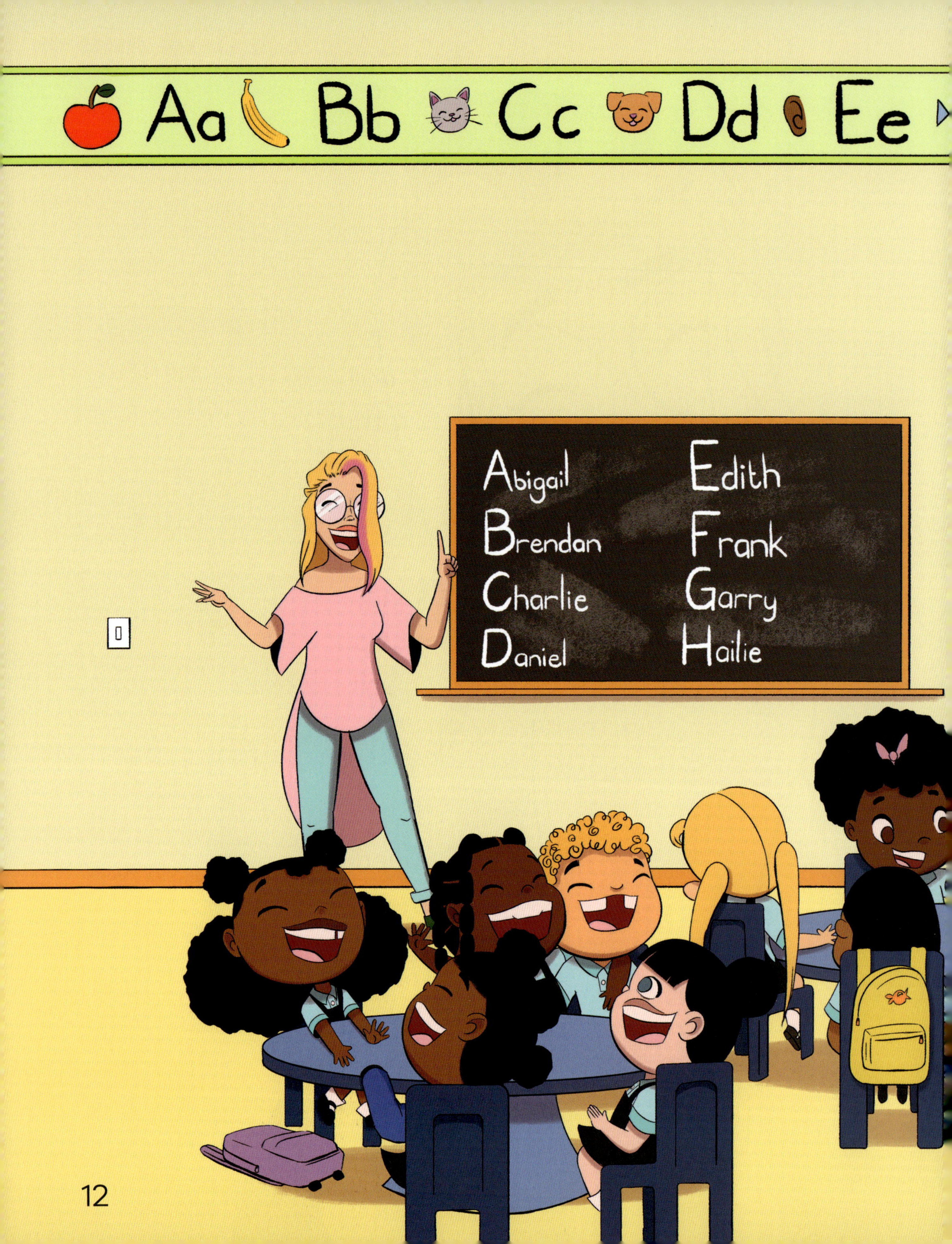
Aa Bb Cc Dd Ee
Abigail
Brendan
Charlie
Daniel
Edith
Frank
Garry
Hailie

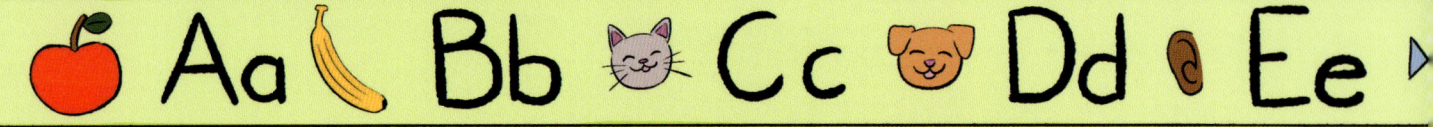

Soon my new classmates arrive,
and the bell rings to start the day.

We learn the alphabet song, and
then Teacher Jess gives us paper and
crayons to draw our favourite things.

When we are finished, she hangs
our pictures on the wall.

Next, she reads us a story.

At first break, we all go out to play.

Break time is the best! I play with **Megan** and **Sofia** and **Jade** and **Ken** …

Mpho and **Mpumi** and **Mbali** and **Ben** …

Mom has packed me a really BIG lunch with all my favourites!

But all my new friends are calling me **Izzy** ...

After break, Teacher Jess calls out our names to make sure we are all back in the classroom.

"Jade?" "Here!"

"Sofia?" "Here!"

"Ken?" "Here!"

"Oh boy, here's this funny name again. Um ... **Izzy?**"

"Here! Sorry, Teacher Jess, but my name is **Isenguye** or Ise," I say.

But she carries on: **"James?"** "Here!"

Why doesn't Teacher Jess want to know my name?

For the rest of the day, Teacher Jess calls me **Izzy**. She gets most of the other kids' names right, except that she calls **Mpumi** "Pumi" and **Mbali** "Ali".

I'm sure she just can't remember all the new names.

My first day of **BIG** school is over,
and my **BIG** sister Amonge comes to pick me up.
I can't wait to tell her about my day!

Meg calls out, "Bye, **Izzy!**"

And so do **Sarah**

and **Karen**

and **Ken**.

I'm so happy my sister can see all my new friends!

"**Isenguye!**" says Amonge.

"Who is Izzy?"

"It's me, of course! My teacher kept on getting my name wrong, even though I corrected her.

I said she could call me Ise for short, but she still got it wrong.

I think my name is too **BIG** for her tongue.

So I think I'll just make it easy and let them call me Izzy."

"No, **Isenguye!** That is not OK! You must never let someone change your name – it takes away your superpowers!"

"My name has superpowers?"

"Yes! Your **BIG name** carries **BIG power!**

Your name means 'God did that'. Mom and Dad didn't make a mistake by naming you **Isenguye** – they were thanking God for blessing them with another precious child!

Your name reminds everyone of God's great gift – **you are a miracle, Isenguye!**

That's your **superpower!**"

On my second day, Teacher Jess calls out the class's names again.

"Ken?" "Here!"

"Izzy?"

I stand up.

"My name is not **Izzy**. My name is **Isenguye**, and it means 'God did that'.

God created a precious miracle that is **ME!** And that's my **SUPERPOWER!** But don't worry, Teacher Jess, I'll teach you how to say it, OK?"

Then **Mandla** stands up ...

"My name is **Mandla** and it means POWER!"

"My name is **Mpumi** and it means to SUCCEED!"

"Yeah, and my name is **Thando** and it means LOVE!"

"And my name is **Mbali** and it means FLOWER."

I like **BIG** school, and I learnt something **BIG** this week.

I learnt that there is power in **my BIG name**, and I won't ever let anyone change it again!

My name is _____

Abeo – Bringer of happiness

Alwande – Let it grow / Let there be more

Amonge – Nurture / Embrace (may God nurture you with love)

Bayanda – They grow / Increase

Bulumko – Wisdom

Cuma – Bloom / Grow

Dimpho – Gift (from God)

Etoma – Life

Isenguye – God did that / It is still Him

Kholofelo – Hope

Khotso – Tranquility / Peace

Kwezi – Morning star

Lesedi – Light

Liyana – Rainfall / Abundance (of blessings)

Lubabalo – Grace / Blessing

Lutho – Valuable gift from God / Destined for greatness

Masana – Morning sun / Sunrise

Mandla – Power

Manqoba – Conqueror

Milisuthando – Bearer of fruits of love

Minenhle – Beautiful day

and it means _____

Mpumi / Mpumelelo – Success

Mulalo – Peace

Netha – Rain / Blessings

Ndumiso – Praise

Noluthando – Love

Nomalanga – Sun

Nqabayomzi – Pillar / Fort of the home

Nsuku – Gold

Nduvho – Praise

Njabulo – Joy

Ntakaso – Joy / Happiness

Owakhe – God's own

Pelontle – Beautiful heart

Rorisang – Gratitude and praise (the name of the Lord)

Sibusiso – Blessing

Simbarashe – Power of God

Shungu – Determination / Ambition

Siphesihle – Beautiful gift

Thapelo – Prayer

Tshepo – Trust

Uyanda – Growth

Zalisa – Fill up empty vessels / Realise a promise

This story was inspired by Owakhe Khanya and Usiphile Isenguye Sinxoto, who would like to dedicate this book to every girl and boy with a special, unique and meaningful name.

Always be proud of your name and never allow anyone make you feel small. We are all so different and beautiful in our own ways. Never let anyone use your difference to make you feel small. There is power in your BIG name!

Learn it. Embrace it. Love it!

© Text Amonge Sinxoto
© David Philip Publishers in typographical layout
© Illustration Lebogang Thato Sekwelenkwe

First edition published in 2022 by David Philip Publishers trading as New Africa Books
Unit 13A, Athlone Industrial Park, 10 Mymoena Crescent, Athlone Industria 2, Cape Town, 7764

All rights reserved. No part of this publication may be produced, stored or introduced into a retrieval system, or transmitted, in any form or by any means (electronic, mechanical, photocopying, recording or otherwise), without the prior written permission of the publisher. Any person who does any unauthorised act in relation to this publication may be liable to criminal prosecution and civil claims for damages.

ISBN: 978-1-4856-3175-0

Editing: Nicola Rijsdijk
Design and Typesetting: Rupert Pluck, iLike Design

Printed by **novus** print, a division of Novus Holdings

David Philip is committed to a sustainable future for our business, our readers and our planet.